Peter's Story of

Jesus

Robert H. Mounce

Copyright 2013 Robert H. Mounce
All rights reserved
ISBN 978-1542548434

Dedicated to Thomas and Laurie Weakley
Faithful Servants of our Lord with Cru at
Western Kentucky University

Peter's Story of Jesus

My name is Peter and I lived many years ago in the land you now call Israel. My brother Andrew and I grew up as fishermen. We lived in the village of Bethsaida in the province of Galilee. One day a man by the name of Jesus came walking by and, noticing that we were about to cast our nets into the water, called out to us, "Come with me and be my disciples. I'll teach you how to fish for men." Although it all happened so quickly, we felt compelled to leave our nets and go with him. That was the beginning of the most unusual three-year period in my life.

I have never known a man like Jesus. As we traveled together throughout Galilee, crowds of people came from all over to hear him teach about the kingdom of God. People were astonished to see him heal all sorts of diseases and even cast out demons. I remember one wild man who used to wander among the tombs at night, shrieking and cutting himself with sharp stones. But that's a story I'll be telling you later.

What I want to do is tell you from personal experience about my time with Jesus. It will be an eyewitness account. My close friend John Mark (in one of my letters I call him "my son" – 1 Peter 5:13) will write it down for me because he is eloquent in Greek and I'm just an uneducated fisherman. Some raise their eyebrows at this so I'm glad that in the second century the famous Bishop of Hierapolis, Papias, wrote that Mark was my "interpreter" and that he "wrote down accurately" what I remembered about Jesus' life and teaching.

Just so you will get an idea of what is in store for you let me mention a couple of episodes in the story you're about to read. Once we were in a storm on the Sea of Galilee and Jesus came walking toward the boat on top of the water. I couldn't believe my eyes. I got so excited that I stepped out of the boat and started toward him. It didn't last long. The waves scared me and I began to sink. Fortunately he laid hold of me and everything turned out okay.

Then there was that time when three of us went with Jesus to the top of a mountain. He was praying and suddenly his face began to shine like the sun and his clothes turned dazzling white. Of course I was the one who just had to say something. But God had the last word — he spoke from heaven and . . . . Well, you'll read all about it. There are so many stories. I'll try not to leave anything out, not even that tragic night when shortly before his crucifixion I denied three times that I knew him.

I'm going to tell you the whole story in the first person so you can experience what actually happened. You'll be one of us. I will tell you a lot of the parables he told us. I'll record all the miracles he did that I can remember. I pray that as I tell you about my years with this remarkable man (in time I came to realize that he was in fact the very son of God) your desire to know him and follow his teachings will be deepened.

Mark One

Here is how the story of my friend Jesus begins. I call the story, "The Good News." In the three years we were together I came to realize that he was the long-awaited Jewish Messiah, the very Son of God. (1:1)

More than 700 years ago God spoke through the prophet Isaiah, saying: "Before I send my Son to earth, I am going to send a messenger who will prepare the way for him. This forerunner will show up in the desert crying out, "Get ready for the Lord. Make the road on which he will come level and smooth." The messenger turned out to be a man by the name of John the Baptizer. He lived in the uninhabited area just north of the Dead Sea. People flocked to him to hear his message ("Repent and God will forgive your sin") and be baptized. People from all over the land of Judea came, even from the capital city of Jerusalem. When they confessed their sins, he baptized them in the Jordan river. (2-5)

John wore a rustic garment woven out of

camel's hair and held together at the waist with a leather strap. For food he lived on grasshoppers and the honey he found in the desert. As he preached to the people, he kept reminding them that someone far greater that he was on his way. John said, "The coming one is so much better than I, that I'm not fit even to get down and take off his sandals. I baptize you with water from this river, but he will baptize you with the Holy Spirit. (6-8)

At that time Jesus was living in the little town of Nazareth near the Sea of Galilee. One day he went to John and was baptized in the Jordan river. As he was coming up out of the water, the heavens suddenly split wide open and God's Spirit, like a dove, came down and settled on him. From heaven God declared, "You are my dear Son, the one I cherish. I am pleased with what you have just done." Then the Spirit made Jesus go into a wilderness area to be tested by Satan. Jesus was there for forty days where wild animals lived, but God's angels took good care of him. (9-13)

Before long John was put in prison for his preaching, so Jesus began to proclaim the same message throughout Galilee. This "Good News" that God wanted people to hear was that the promised time had arrived and that God was about to establish his reign on earth. As John had said, "Repent!" It was crucial that people believe what Jesus was telling them. (14-15)

One day Jesus was walking along the shore of the Lake of Galilee when he saw me, Peter, and my brother Andrew casting a net into the sea (we were fishermen). He called to us, "Come with me and I'll show you how to fish for people." Without hesitation we put down our nets and went with him. We hadn't gone very far until Jesus saw two more brothers, James and John, the sons of Zebedee. They were in their boat repairing some nets that had been torn. When Jesus called they got up, left their father in the boat with his hired men, and came with us. (16-20)

Before long we arrived at the town of Capernaum. When the Sabbath came, Jesus went into the local synagogue and began to teach. The people were astonished at his teaching because, unlike the teachers of religious law, he taught with authority; he didn't merely quote what others had said. All of a sudden a man possessed by an evil spirit jumped up and yelled, "You, Jesus from Nazareth! What are you trying to do? Have you come to destroy us? I know about you — you're a messenger from God."

Jesus rebuked the evil spirit, saying, "That's enough out of you! Come out of that man!" The evil spirit threw the man into convulsions; then, screaming at the top of its voice, came out of the man. Everyone who saw it was amazed. They began to ask one another, "What's this all about? It has to be something brand new! With what authority he orders the evil spirits and they obey without questioning!"

So the news about Jesus spread quickly throughout Galilee. (21-28)

Jesus, along with James and John, left the synagogue and went straight to where my brother Andrew and I lived. When we arrived, Jesus was told that my mother-in-law couldn't get out of bed because of a high fever. Jesus went to where she was lying, took her hand in his and raised her to a sitting position. The fever suddenly disappeared and, as the lady of the house, she began to serve refreshments to her guests. (29-31)

That evening after sunset, when the Sabbath was over, the villagers began to bring to Jesus everyone who was sick, even some who were possessed by demons. The whole town crowded around the door to see what was going on. Jesus cured a great number of those who were sick with various kinds of diseases. He also cast out many demons, but he wouldn't allow them to say a word, because they knew who he really was. (32-34)

Very early the next morning, while it was still dark, Jesus got up, left the house and went out where he could be by himself and pray. Later, I and some others went to look for him. When we found him, we said, "Everybody is looking for you."

Jesus answered, "We need to move on to other towns in the area so they can hear the Good News as well. You know of course, that's why I came." So he went everywhere throughout Galilee, proclaiming the Good News in their synagogues and casting out demons. (35-39)

One day a man with a terrible skin disease came to Jesus for help. Falling on his knees, he exclaimed, "If only you were willing you could make this leprosy go away."

Filled with compassion, Jesus reached out his hand and touched the man. "I am willing," he said. "May your skin be like new." At once the leprosy disappeared and his skin was like new. Then Jesus sent him on his way with a stern warning that he not tell others what had happened. "Don't tell anyone about this," Jesus said. "Instead, go to Jerusalem and there you can be examined by a priest. Offer the sacrifice prescribed by Moses that officially declares those who have been healed, then everyone will know you no longer have leprosy. But instead of following Jesus' instructions, the man went out and began to tell everyone everywhere what had happened. As a result, Jesus could no longer go openly into any town. Rather, he had to stay out where he would less likely attract attention. However, people kept coming out to him from everywhere. (40-45)

Mark Two

After several days, Jesus returned to my home in Capernaum. The news got around quickly and before long so many people had crowded into the house that there was no more room. There was no place to sit or stand, even outside the door within hearing distance. While Jesus was explaining the message of salvation to them, four men arrived carrying a paralytic. They couldn't get inside because of the crowd so they climbed up on the roof, opened up a hole right above Jesus and lowered the man, stretcher and all. When Jesus saw this remarkable act of faith he said to the paralytic, "My son, your sins are forgiven!" (1- 5)

Mingling with the crowd were some teachers of religious law who reasoned to themselves, "How does he dare speak like that? That's blasphemy! No one but God can forgive sins!"

Right away Jesus was aware of what they were thinking, so he asked, "Why are you pondering ideas like that? Tell me; is it easier to say to this paralyzed man, "Your sins are forgiven," or to say to him, "Stand up, pick up your stretcher and walk?" So you will see that I, the Son of Man, have authority here on earth to forgive sins, I now say to this paralytic, "Stand up, pick up your stretcher and go home!" Right before their eyes the paralyzed man rose to his feet, reached down to pick up his stretcher, then walked out of the house right through the crowd.

Everyone was astonished. Praising God, they exclaimed, "We've never seen anything like this before!" (6-12)

Once again Jesus went out along the lake and began to teach all those who came to hear him. As he walked along, he saw a local customs officer Levi, son of Alphaeus, sitting where he collected taxes. "Come with me," said Jesus. "Be my disciple." So Levi got up and went with him.

Later on Jesus was having a meal in Levi's house. We disciples were there along with a number of tax collectors and other religious outcasts who were followers of Jesus. When the teachers of religious law within the Pharisee party saw Jesus eating with people that they considered ceremonial unclean, they asked us, "Why in the world does your teacher eat with tax collectors and other religious outcasts?"

Jesus overheard this and said to them, "It is sick people who need a doctor, not the healthy. I've not come to call to repentance those who think they are righteous, but those who know they are sinners." (13-17)

On one occasion some of John the Baptist's disciples who were trying to live by Pharisaic rules were keeping a fast. Some people came to Jesus and asked, "Why do John's disciples join the Pharisees in fasting, but yours do not?"

Jesus replied, "Surely wedding guests do not fast as long as the bridegroom is still with them. The day will come when the bridegroom is no longer with them and that's when they can fast." (18-20)

"No one uses a piece of new cloth in mending a tear in an old garment. If they did, the new patch would shrink and tear away from the garment, leaving it worse than before. And no one pours new wine into old wineskins. If they did, the fermenting wine would burst the wineskins and both wine and skins would be lost. No, new wine belongs in brand new wineskins." (21-22)

One Sabbath day Jesus and the rest of us were out walking and our route took us past a grain field. As we made our way, we began to pick some heads of wheat (as allowed by OT law). Some Pharisees, who were watching, said to Jesus, "Look at them! Why are they doing what is strictly forbidden on the Sabbath?"

Jesus responded, "Have you never read what David did when he and his men were hungry and needed something to eat — how he went into the house of God and, although it was against the law, ate the sacred bread and even gave some to his companions?" (This was during the days when Abiathar was high priest and no one except priests was allowed to eat the sacred loaves.)

"So you see," said Jesus, "the Sabbath was made for our benefit; we weren't created for it. That is why the Son of Man is Lord even of the Sabbath." (23-28)

Mark Three

After that Jesus went back to Capernaum. On the Sabbath he went to the synagogue and a man with a paralyzed hand was there. Some Pharisees were watching Jesus carefully to see if he would restore the crippled hand. If he did, they could accuse him of working on the Sabbath. So Jesus said to the man with the paralyzed hand, "Come over here so everyone can see you." Then he said to his critics, "Does our law allow us to do what is right on the Sabbath or what is wrong? Shall I heal this man's hand or leave it paralyzed?"

The Pharisees had nothing to say. Jesus looked around at them with disgust. Grieved by their lack of compassion, he said to the man, "Stretch out your hand." The man stretched out his hand, and once again he could flex his fingers. The Pharisees left the synagogue and immediately began plotting with the followers of Herod how to get rid of Jesus. (1-6)

We all left Capernaum and went down to lake Galilee. We were followed by a huge crowd of people. They came from Galilee, Jerusalem,

Idumea, the region east of the Jordan river, as well as the area to the north around the cities of Tyre and Sidon. They came to Jesus from everywhere because they had heard about the miracles he was doing. Jesus told us to keep a small boat available in case he was in danger of being crushed by the crowd. (He had healed so many, and the sick kept crowding in to touch him.) Whenever the evil spirits saw him, they would fall before him, shrieking, "You are the Son of God!" But Jesus warned them repeatedly not to reveal who he was. (7-12)

Then Jesus went up into the hills and called together the twelve of us that he had chosen to be with him. We were designated "apostles" and were to be his close companions. In time we would be sent out to proclaim the Good News. "You will have the authority to cast out demons," he told us. I was one of the twelve, and Jesus gave me the name "Peter" (although my Hebrew name is Simon.) The others were James and his brother John (they were sons of Zebedee, and Jesus named them Boanerges, "Sons of Thunder"), Andrew, Philip, Bartholomew, Matthew, Thomas,

James (the son of Alphaeus), Thaddaeus, Simon (the Zealot), and Judas Iscariot (who later betrayed Jesus.) (13-19)

After this, we went back to my house in Capernaum and once again a crowd gathered. It was so large that we didn't even have time to eat. Back in Nazareth, Jesus' family had heard what was going on, so they came to Capernaum to do something about it. They thought Jesus had lost his mind. The teachers of religious law who had come from Jerusalem were claiming, "He's possessed by Beelzebul! It is Satan, the ruler of demons, who has given him the power to cast out demons."

So Jesus called them over and posed the question, "How can Satan cast out Satan? If a country divides itself into warring groups it will soon collapse. In the same way, if a family fights among itself, it will self destruct. So if Satan's kingdom rebels against itself and is divided, it cannot last — its end is near. No one can break into a strong man's house and carry off his possessions unless first they have tied him up. Only then can they rob his house.

I tell you the truth, people can be forgiven for every sinful word they have ever spoken, even blasphemies; but whoever blasphemes the Holy Spirit will never be forgiven. That person is guilty of an eternal sin." Jesus said this because his opponents were claiming that he was possessed by an evil spirit. (20-30)

About that time the mother and brothers of Jesus arrived at my house. They remained outside and asked that Jesus join them there. Inside the house, the crowd gathered around Jesus told him, "Your mother and brothers are outside asking for you."

Jesus responded, "Who, in fact, is my mother; and who are my brothers?" Then he looked at those around him and said, "You people right here are my mother and my true brothers! Whoever does what pleases God has become my brother, my sister, my mother. (31-35)

Mark Four

Once again Jesus went down to the lake and continued to teach the crowd that had gathered there. So many had come to hear him that he decided to get into a boat and push out a short distance. To the people on shore he taught many spiritual truths using stories from everyday life. Here are some of his parables: (1-2)

"Once there as a man who went out into his field to plant a crop. As he scattered the seeds, some fell along the edge of the field where the ground hadn't been plowed. It was easy for birds to fly in and snatch them off the hard ground. Other seeds fell on the thin layer of soil covering hard rock. They sprouted quickly because the soil was so thin. But when hot weather came the plants withered because their roots were shallow. Some seeds fell into thorns that grew quickly and choked the young plants so they were unable to produce grain. But other seeds fell on good soil and the plants sprouted and grew. Some produced thirty grains per plant, others sixty, some one hundred." Jesus warned the crowd,

"Whoever has ears to hear should pay attention to what I have said." (3-9)

Later on when the crowd had left, a few remained to be with Jesus. We, the Twelve, were there as well. When asked about the parables, Jesus said, "The secret of the kingdom of God has been revealed to you, but to those on the outside (like those who had just left), my words are no more than stories. The Old Testament prophecies are being fulfilled that say, 'They look and look but see nothing; they listen and listen but don't understand; if they did, they would change their ways and be forgiven.'" (10-12)

Then Jesus said, "Don't you understand the parable of the sower? If you can't understand this simple parable, how can you understand all the others? Let me explain. The farmer sows the seed, that is, the message of the kingdom. Some of it falls on the hard ground alongside the field. The hard ground represents people who hear but immediately Satan comes and carries away what they have just heard. The seeds sown on shallow soil are people who, when they hear the message, receive it immediately with joy; but since they don't have deep roots, they last only a short time. When trouble comes and they are persecuted for what they believe, they will deny their faith and quit. The seeds that fall among the thorns are people who hear the message but worldly concerns, the seductive lure of wealth, and all their other passions come in and choke the message so that it produces nothing. But the seeds sown on good soil are those who hear and accept the message. Some produce a harvest of thirty-to-one, others sixty, and some even one hundred-to-one." (13-20)

Then Jesus asked, "Would it make sense to light a lamp and then hide it under a basket or under the bed? Of course not! Lamps belong on lamp stands. Nothing is hidden that won't be disclosed, and nothing is kept secret that won't be brought to light. Whoever has ears to hear should pay attention to what I have said."

Then Jesus added, "Pay attention to what you hear because the more carefully you listen the more you will understand. Careful listening is rewarded with greater understanding. Whoever listens carefully to my teaching will understand even more, but as for those who are not paying attention, what little they do know will be taken away from them." (21-25)

Jesus went on to say, "Let me tell you another story so you'll understand what the kingdom of God is like. A farmer takes some seeds and scatters them in a field. Then, night and day, whether the farmer is asleep or awake, the seeds begin to sprout and grow although he doesn't have the faintest idea how it all happens. It is the soil all by itself that produces the crop; first it sends up the stalk, then the head appears, and finally the head is filled with grain. As soon as the grain is ripe, the farmer takes his sickle and starts to reap because harvest time has come." (26-29)

"How else," pondered Jesus, "can I describe to you the kingdom of God? What kind of picture can I draw so you will see what it is like? Here's one. The kingdom of God is like a tiny mustard seed. It's the smallest of all seeds, but when planted in the ground it sprouts and in time becomes the largest plant in the garden. It grows so large that birds can come and build their nests in its shade."

Jesus used many other parables like these to teach the message to people in so far as each was able to understand. In fact, he always used parables to teach the crowds, but when he was alone with us, he explained more fully what they meant. (30-34)

That very evening Jesus said to us, "Let's cross over to the other side of the lake." So we left the crowds and set out in the boat in which Jesus was already sitting. (There were other boats nearby.) Suddenly a fierce storm arose and the waves began to break over into the boat and fill it with water. However, Jesus remained sound asleep in the stern with his head on a boat cushion.

We woke him up, shouting, "Master, don't you care that we're about to drown?"

So Jesus got up, rebuked the wind, and said to the sea, "Quiet now! Settle down!" Immediately the wind died down and a great calm settled over the lake. Then Jesus said to us, "Why were you so frightened? Are you still without faith?"

We were terrified by what Jesus had just

done. "Who is this man?" we asked one another. "Even the wind and the sea do whatever he tells them." (35-41)

Mark Five

Soon we came to land on the north shore of Lake Galilee, in the territory of the Gerasenes. No sooner had Jesus stepped out of the boat than a man possessed by an evil spirit approached him. This man lived in the burial caves. He was so strong that no one could tie him down, not even with chains.

More than once the townspeople had bound him hand and foot but he would snap the chains they had put on his wrists and break the shackles on his feet. No one was able to restrain him. Day and night he would wander among the tombs, howling and gnashing himself with sharp stones. When from a distance the man saw Jesus, he ran to him and fell to the ground. "Go away Jesus!" he shrieked, "Leave me alone, you son of the Most High God! Swear to God that you won't torment me!" (Jesus had already said to the spirit, "Come out of the man, you evil spirit!) (1-8)

"Tell me your name!" demanded Jesus.

The evil spirit answered, "My name is Legion,

for there are so many of us." Then the spirit kept begging Jesus not to send them off to some far away place. It so happened that there was a huge herd of pigs feeding on a nearby hillside. "Send us to those pigs," begged the evil spirits; "Let us go into them." Jesus gave them permission and the evil spirits came out of the man and went into the pigs. The pigs, all two thousand of them, rushed madly down the steep bank and into the water where they drowned. The men who tended the pigs ran and told the local villagers and others what had happened. When they arrived, they saw the man they knew to be possessed by a horde of demons, now sitting beside Jesus, fully clothed and in his right mind. They were frightened out of their mind. The people who had watched the demons being expelled and go into the pigs described it all to the crowd, whose reaction was to plead with Jesus to get out of their country. (9-17)

As we were getting a boat ready to shove off, the man who had been possessed by demons begged to go with us, but Jesus wouldn't let him. Instead, he told the man, "Go home to your family and tell them how much the Lord has done for you — the kindness he has shown to you." The man went away alright but not to his own home, but to a region called the Decapolis ("Ten Towns") where he told everyone what Jesus had done for him. And they were all amazed. (18-20)

Jesus had no sooner gotten into the boat and crossed to the other side, than a large crowd gathered around him on the shore. Among the crowd was Jairus, one of the officials in the synagogue at Capernaum. Coming to Jesus, he fell at his feet and pled earnestly for his little daughter who was dying. "Please come and place your hands on her so she will get well and live!" So Jesus went with Jairus, followed by a mob of people that kept crowding around them. (21-24)

In the group was a woman who had suffered for twelve years from severe bleeding. She had gone through a great deal under the care of many doctors, and had spent everything she had, but not gotten any better. In fact she was worse than before. She'd heard what Jesus was able to do, so she slipped up from behind and touched his robe, thinking, "If I can only touch his robe, I'll get well."

Immediately the bleeding stopped, and she could feel in her body that she'd been healed.

Jesus immediately sensed that healing power had gone out of him, so he turned to the crowd and asked, "Who touched my robe?"

We said to him, "Master, look at all the people crowding around you; how could you ask, 'Who touched me?'" But Jesus kept looking around to see who had done it. When the woman realized what had happened to her, she went back to Jesus, frightened and trembling. She fell at his feet and admitted that she had touched him even though being ceremonially unclean it was forbidden.

Jesus said to her, "My daughter, your faith has made you well. Your time of suffering is now over and you can mingle with others." (25-34)

While Jesus was speaking to the woman, some people from the house of Jairus arrived and reported to him, "Your daughter has died! There's no longer any reason to bother the teacher."

Overhearing this, Jesus turned to Jairus and said, "Don't be afraid, just believe." No one in the crowd was to go with him any further. I was the only one, along with James and John that was permitted to go further. When we arrived at the home of the synagogue official, we were met with absolute chaos — loud crying and unrestrained wailing.

Jesus went inside and asked, "Why all the commotion? Why all the weeping? The child has not died, she is simply asleep." The crowd ridiculed him with laughter. So he sent them all outside and taking the father and mother with him, went to the child's room. (We three disciples went as well.) Then Jesus took the child by the hand and said to her in Aramaic, "Talitha Koum!" which means, "Little girl, get up." Immediately she got out of bed and began to walk around. Everyone there was absolutely amazed. Jesus gave strict orders to tell no one what had happened. Then he encouraged the parents to give her something to eat. (35-43)

Mark Six

After this we left the territory of the Gerasenes and went to Nazareth, Jesus' hometown. When the Sabbath came, he went to the synagogue to teach. Many of those who heard what he had to say were astounded. "Where did he learn all that?" they asked. "What new insight has been given to him? How is he able to perform such miracles? Isn't this fellow simply the carpenter, the son of Mary? We all know his brothers — James, Joseph, Judas, and Simon. His sisters live right here in town, don't they?" So those who heard what Jesus had to say were deeply offended. He responded by reminding them of the ancient saying that prophets are respected everywhere except in their own country. Because they wouldn't believe, Jesus was unable to perform even a single miracle there — except he did lay his hands on a few of the sick and healed them. He was amazed that they would not believe, so he left Nazareth and went elsewhere, teaching as he went. (1-6)

Jesus called us together in preparation for

sending us out on a mission, two by two. We were given authority to cast out evil spirits. He told us not to take any of the normal provisions for such a journey, like a staff, food, a traveling bag, or money. It was okay to wear sandals but we shouldn't take any extra clothes. He told us that in whatever house we were staying, we should remain there until we left that village. However, if the people of the village were not cordial and refused to listen to us, then we were to leave. As we left town, we were to shake the dust of the town off our feet. That would serve as a warning to them. So we left on our mission, telling everyone we met that they should repent. (7-13)

By this time, Herod Antipas (who was regarded as king, although his father Augustus was the ruling monarch) had become aware of Jesus' reputation. Some people were saying, "He must be John the Baptist raised from the dead; how else can you explain his power to perform such miracles?"

Others were saying, "No, he is the prophet Elijah."

Still others were saying, "Well, he certainly is a prophet; he's just like one of the great prophets of old." (14-16)

Herod himself sent soldiers to arrest John. He ordered them to bind John with chains and throw him into prison. This was to please his wife Herodias, whom he had married even though she was already married to his brother Phillip. John the Baptist had told Herod more than once, "It's against God's law for you to marry the wife of your brother." So Herodias nursed a grudge against John and would have liked to put him to death, but wasn't able because Herod had a high regard for him. Herod knew that John was a just and righteous man, so he granted him protection. He enjoyed listening to him talk, but every time he heard him, he came away thoroughly confused. (17-20)

It was on Herod's birthday that Herodias finally got her chance. The king was giving a big party and had invited the nobles of his royal court, the military commanders and other prominent figures in Galilee. When the festivities were well underway, the daughter of Herodias came in and performed a dance for the group. This greatly pleased Herod and his guests. To the young girl the king blurted out, "Wow! After a dance like that you can ask me for whatever you want. Just name it and its yours."

He kept promising her, with an oath, that he would give her whatever she asked for, even up to half of his kingdom. So she left the room and asked her mother, "What should I ask him for?"

Herodias was ready with an answer: "The head of John the Baptist."

Without hesitation the girl hurried back to the party and said to the king, "I want the head of John the Baptist, right now, on a tray."

When Herod realized what he had done he was filled with remorse. But because he had made the promise with an oath — to say nothing of his reputation with the guests — he had no option but to grant her what she wanted. So without delay he sent one of his bodyguards to carry out the task. Serving as executioner, the guard went to the prison, beheaded John and brought the head on a tray to the girl. She handed it over to Herodias, her mother. When John's disciples heard what had happened, they came for the body and laid it in a tomb. (21-29)

We returned from our mission trip and met with Jesus to report all that we had done and what we had taught. So many people crowded around us that we didn't have time even to eat. Jesus said, "Let's slip away to some quiet place so you can get a good rest." So we left by boat to a place where we could be alone. But there was no way to get there without being seen. Many from the surrounding towns recognized us and ran along the shore arriving there ahead of us.

When we landed, Jesus stepped out of the boat and, seeing the large crowd, was filled with compassion. They were like lost sheep — sheep without a shepherd. This so moved him that he began immediately to teach them all sorts of important truths.

Later in the afternoon we went to him and said, "We're in a remote area and its already getting late. Tell the crowds to go to the farms around here or the villages and buy themselves something to eat."

His answer came as a surprise, "No, you yourselves are to give them whatever food they need."

We asked, "How can we do that? It would take more than six months' wages to buy enough bread for a crowd this size."

Jesus asked us, "How many loaves do you have in the boat? Go check it out."

When we came back we said, "We've only got five loaves of bread — plus a couple of little fish."

Then Jesus told us to have all the people sit down on the grass in groups of fifty or a hundred. This they did in an orderly fashion. It was spring and the grass was green. Jesus took the loaves of flat bread and the little fish, and raising his eyes to heaven gave thanks for the Father's provision. Then he broke the bread into pieces and handed it to us to distribute among the people. He also divided the fish so all could share. Everyone ate until they were full. When we picked up what they didn't eat, the scraps filled twelve baskets. All in all, some five thousand men plus their families were fed on that occasion. (30-44)

Jesus had us get back in the boat and return to Bethsaida on the far side of the lake. Meanwhile, he himself dispersed the crowd, wishing them a safe trip home. Then he went up into the hills to pray.

As the night wore on we were nearing the middle of the lake and Jesus was standing alone on shore. He could see us straining at the oars against the high wind and heavy sea. In the early hours of the morning he came toward us walking on the water. It looked to us like he would pass us by. When we saw him walking on the water we were terrified — every last one of us. We cried out, "It's a ghost!"

Immediately Jesus spoke to us saying, "Take courage! It is I. Don't be afraid." Then he climbed into the boat with us, and the wind died down. His power over wind and wave was amazing to us since our hearts were still too dull to understand a miracle even like the feeding of the five thousand.

We came to shore at Gennesaret and tied up our boat. When we got out, the people recognized Jesus at once. They hurried through the entire region and carried the sick to wherever Jesus was said to be — in some village, or town, or rural area. They would lay down their sick in open places and beg Jesus to let the sick touch the edge of his robe. Everyone who managed to touch him was healed. (45-55)

Mark Seven

One day some experts in religious law came from Jerusalem, joined some local Pharisees and came to see Jesus. They noticed that some of us were eating with what they call "unclean hands," that is, not ceremonially cleansed. (The Jews, especially the Pharisees, do not eat unless they have washed their hands according to the ritual prescribed by the elders. When they return from the market place, that ritual is carried out on the entire body. They follow all sorts of rules established by tradition such as the proper way to wash cups, pots, copper bowls and even dining couches.) So they asked Jesus, "Why is it that your disciples have no respect for the tradition of the elders? Look at them; they are eating with unclean hands!"

Jesus answered, "Isaiah was right when he looked into the future and said of you hypocrites, 'This people honors me with their lips but their hearts are far from me. Their worship is worthless, teaching their own regulations as though they were the laws of God.' You people ignore God's law and follow your own traditions."

Jesus continued, saying, "You circumvent the commands of God in order to establish your own tradition. For example, through Moses God commanded, 'Honor your father and your mother,' and, 'Whoever speaks disrespectfully of his father or mother must be put to death.' But you teach that if a person says to his father or mother, 'What ever I might have given you is Korban (that is, "promised to God"), then they no longer have to help their parents in need. That is how you manipulate your tradition so as to nullify the word of God. And you do lots of other things like that as well." (1-13)

Then Jesus gathered the crowd around him and said, "Listen to me, all of you, and understand what I'm about to say. No one is defiled by what comes in from the outside. It's what comes out of people that makes them ritually unclean."

When Jesus left the crowd and went indoors, we asked him what he meant by that. "Are you as slow to catch on as the crowd outside," he asked? "Don't you understand that you can't be defiled by something entering your body from the outside?

That's because it doesn't go into the inner man, but into the stomach and from there, into the sewer." (By saying this, Jesus declared every kind of food clean.) Then he added, "A person is defiled by what comes out of him. It is from the inner man, the heart, that come the evil inclinations that lead to sexual immorality, theft, murder, adultery, greed, wickedness, deceit, lustful desires, selfishness, slander, arrogance, and lack of moral judgment. All these evil things come from within and they are what defile a person." (14-23)

From there Jesus went north to the area around the city of Tyre. He decided to stay indoors to escape notice but it didn't work. A Gentile woman, Syrophoenician by birth, had a young daughter who was possessed by an evil spirit. The woman heard that Jesus was nearby, so without hesitation she came, fell at his feet, and asked him to drive out the demon. Jesus put her off, saying, "It wouldn't be right for me to take food that should go to my own children (the Jews) first, and throw it out so the dogs (the Gentiles) can get it."

Using his own argument, she responded, "That's absolutely right, Sir; but isn't it also true that the puppies that play under the children's table get the crumbs that fall to the floor?"

"Touché!" answered Jesus. "When you arrive back home you'll find that the demon has left your daughter." And that's exactly what happened! When the Gentile woman arrived home, the demon was nowhere to be found and the little girl was sleeping quietly in bed. (24-30)

After this, Jesus left Tyre and returned to Galilee and the Decapolis (the Ten Towns) by way of Sidon. Once there, some people brought a man to him who was unable to hear and hardly able to talk. They urged Jesus to lay hands on him and heal him. Jesus took him aside where they could be alone. Then he spit on his fingers and touched the man's ears and tongue. Looking up to heaven, he said with a deep sigh, "Ephphatha" (Aramaic for "Open up!") Immediately the man was able to hear, his speech impediment disappeared and he began to speak clearly.

The crowd, which had gathered, was dumbfounded and exclaimed, "Everything he does is remarkable! He makes it possible for the deaf to hear and the tongue-tied to speak!" Jesus warned them to tell no one what had happened, but the more he insisted the more they spread the news. (31-37)

Mark Eight

Not many days later the crowd that was following us realized they had run out of food. So Jesus said to us, his disciples, "I am so sorry for these people because they have been with us now for three days and have nothing left to eat. Some of them have come so far that if I send them away hungry they will collapse on the way home."

"But how could we possibly come up with enough food in this deserted place to feed so many?" we queried.

"How many loaves do you have?"

"Seven," we answered.

So Jesus told the crowd to sit down on the ground. Then he took our seven loaves and, after giving thanks to God, handed them back to us and we distributed them among the crowd. We also had a few pieces of fish, so after Jesus had blessed them, we passed them out as well. The crowd of about four thousand had all they wanted to eat, and when we picked up what was left over, we filled seven good sized baskets. Then Jesus sent the crowd on their way, and without waiting got into the boat with us. We headed northwest across the lake to the district of Dalmanutha. (1-10)

Upon landing, some local Pharisees showed up and challenged Jesus. "Show us some miraculous sign," they insisted. "Make God respond from heaven so we can be convinced of your authority."

Hearing this, Jesus gave a deep sigh and said, "Why is it that you people keep demanding yet another miracle? I tell you the truth, no further evidence will be given." Then Jesus left the gathering, got into the boat and headed back with us to the other side of the lake. (11-13)

We had forgotten to bring a supply of food and had only a single loaf of bread. As we were crossing, Jesus warned us in no uncertain terms, "Beware of the yeast (the powerful influence) of the Pharisees! Watch out for Herod as well."

We said to one another, "He must be talking

about yeast because we forgot to bring bread."

Aware of our confusion, Jesus asked, "Why are you discussing the lack of bread? Don't you understand what I am talking about? Are you clueless? You've got eyes — can't you see? And ears — can't you hear? Or have you forgotten what happened when I fed five thousand people with five loaves? How many baskets did you fill with those scraps?"

"Twelve," we answered.

"And when I satisfied the hunger of four thousand with only seven loaves, how much did you pick up?"

"Seven baskets-full" we confessed.

"So," concluded Jesus, "can't you see what God is doing right now in your midst?" (14-21)

When we landed near Bethsaida some people brought a blind man to Jesus. They wanted desperately for Jesus to touch him so he could see again. Jesus took the blind man by the hand and led him outside the village. After spitting in the man's eyes and touching them with his hands, he asked him, "Do you see anything yet?"

Looking around, the man said, "I see what seems to be people walking around; they look like trees." Once again Jesus touched the man's eyes with his hands. This time the blind man's eyesight was perfectly restored and everything became clear and distinct. Jesus sent him home but warned him to by-pass the village. (22-26)

From there we set out to visit the various villages around the regional capital of Caesarea Philippi. As we were on our way, Jesus asked, "Tell me, who do people say I am?"

"Some say you are John the Baptizer," we answered. "Others say you are Elijah or one of the other prophets."

"But you," he asked; who do you say I am?"

I, Peter, spoke up and said, "You are the Christ, the promised Messiah." Jesus warned us not to tell this to anyone. (27-30)

At this point Jesus began to teach us that the Son of Man, was destined to suffer greatly. He said, "I will be rejected by the elders, the chief priests and the teachers of religious law. They will go so far as to put me to death, but after three days I will rise again."

Since Jesus was speaking quite openly about this new stage in his ministry, I took him aside and began to rebuke him for what he said. Jesus turned so as to look at all of us then, reprimanding me, said, "Get away from me, Satan! You are thinking like a man of this world, not like a citizen of heaven." (31-33)

When the crowd had joined us, Jesus began to teach, saying, "Whoever would be a follower of mine must renounce his life, take up his cross and join me on the road to execution. Whoever lives his life for himself will lose it, but whoever sacrifices it for my sake and the sake of the gospel, will save it. Think about it: What good would it be to win the whole world if it cost you your life? There is nothing as valuable as life. If a person is ashamed of me in this rebellious and sinful world, then I will be ashamed of them when

I am gloriously enthronement in heaven. (34-38)

Mark Nine

Jesus went on to say, "I tell you the truth, some of you who are standing right here will, before you die, experience the powerful reign of God.

Six days later Jesus took three of us (James, John and me) and hiked way up a mountain where we could be alone. Once there, Jesus was transfigured before our very eyes. His clothing became dazzling white. Nothing this side of heaven could have made them so brilliant. Suddenly the prophet Elijah was there — and Moses as well — and they were talking with Jesus!

I simply had to say something, so I blurted out, "Rabbi. It's wonderful to be here. Let's set up three shelters — one for you, one for Moses and another for Elijah! (We were in awe and I didn't know what to say.)" Just then a cloud overshadowed us and from the cloud came a voice, "This is my Son, the one I love. Listen to him." We hid our faces and after a moment, when we looked again, Moses and Elijah were no longer there. We were alone with Jesus and everything had returned to normal. (1-8)

As we were coming down the mountain, Jesus told us in no uncertain terms that we should not tell anyone what we had seen until he, the Son Man, had risen from the dead. So we kept all this to ourselves, although we did discuss what "rising from the dead" could possibly mean. We asked Jesus, "Why do the teachers of religious law insist that Elijah must return before the 'awesome Day of the Lord?'"

He answered, "Elijah does come first and gets everything ready. But why does Scripture say that the Son of Man must suffer greatly and be treated with contempt? I tell you that Elijah has already come and, just as it is written in Scripture, they treated him just as they pleased." (9-13)

After coming down the mountain, we saw the other disciples surrounded by a large crowd, and some teachers of the law arguing with them. When the crowd saw Jesus they were thrilled and came running as fast as they could to greet him.

To the teachers of religious law, Jesus said, "What have you been arguing about with my disciples?"

A man in the crowd answered, "Teacher, I brought my son to you because he's under the control of an evil spirit and can't speak. It seizes him and hurls him to the ground. My son foams at the mouth, grinds his teeth and becomes rigid from head to foot. I asked your disciples to cast the demon out, but they couldn't do it."

To those standing by, Jesus exclaimed, "You unbelieving people! How much longer must I be here with you? How much longer do I have to put up with you? Bring me the boy." So they brought the boy, but the instant the evil spirit saw Jesus, it threw the boy into a convulsion causing him to collapse on the ground and roll around foaming at the mouth. "How long has this been going on" asked Jesus?

"Ever since he was a little boy," answered the father. "Time and time again the evil spirit has tried to destroy him by throwing him into fire or holding him under water. If you can do anything, please show compassion and help us.

"If I can?" Jesus responded. "Nothing is impossible for the one who believes."

Instantly the father cried out. "I do believe; help me never to doubt again!"

Since the crowd was now quickly gathering around him, Jesus knew the time to act had come. He rebuked the spirit, saying, "You evil spirit who makes this boy unable to hear or speak, I order you to come out of him right now and never return!"

The evil spirit screamed in opposition, but, after throwing the boy into violent convulsions, came out of him. The boy appeared so much like a corpse that those standing there thought he was dead. But Jesus took him by the hand and helped him to his feet.

We left the scene and went indoors. Going to Jesus in private we asked, "Why couldn't we cast out the evil spirit?"

Jesus answered, "This kind is cast out only by prayer." (14-29)

We moved on from there and made our way through Galilee. Jesus didn't want others to know where we were because it would take time for us to understand fully what he meant when he said, "The Son of Man will be delivered into the hands of men who will put him to death, but after three days I will rise from the dead." At the time we didn't understand what he was talking about and were afraid to ask him. (30-32)

When we arrived back home in Capernaum and had gone inside, Jesus asked, "What were you discussing on the way? No one said a word because we had been arguing about which of us was the greatest, and we knew that was wrong. At that point Jesus sat down as our teacher and told us to gather around. He said to us, "Whoever wants to be first must place himself last and serve everyone else."

Then he took one of the children playing there, gave him a hug, and placed him before us. "You see this child?" asked Jesus. "I made him feel good about being here. Whoever welcomes others in this way welcomes me, and whoever welcomes me, welcomes not only me but also the One who sent me." (33-38)

One day John went to Jesus and said, "Master, we saw a man casting out demons in your name. We told him to stop because he wasn't one of us."

"That wasn't right," said Jesus, "because no one who can perform a miracle by using my name will soon after that be able to speak evil of me. Whoever is not against us, is for us. I assure you that whoever gives you a drink of water because you bear Christ's name will certainly never lose his reward.

"If anyone should damage the faith of one of my followers, it would have been better for him to have had a huge millstone tied around his neck and been thrown into the sea. If your hand is damaging your faith, cut it off. It is far better to go through life with one hand than to burn in the unquenchable fires of hell with two. Or if your foot is damaging your faith, cut it off. Better to go through life as an amputee than to be thrown in hell with two feet. Or if your eye is damaging your faith, get rid of it. Better to go through life with only one eye than to have two and be thrown into hell 'where the maggot never dies and the fire never goes out.'" (39-48)

"Everyone will be tested by suffering. Salt is good, but if it loses its tang how do you restore it? Salt preserves your relationships and helps you to be at peace with one another." (49-50)

Mark Ten

Jesus left Capernaum and traveled south into the region of Judea and the land east of the Jordan river. Once again he attracted crowds of people and as always he began to teach them. Some Pharisees, intending to trap him, asked, "Does our law allow a man to divorce his wife?"

"What did Moses say about that in the law?" Jesus replied.

They answered, "Moses allowed a man to simply hand his wife a written notice of divorce and send her away."

"He allowed that, of course," countered Jesus, "because you people are so hard of heart. It wasn't that way in the beginning when God created the world. As scripture says, 'God made them male and female.' That's why a man will leave his parents and bond with his wife. No longer are they two separate beings – they have become one. Since it is God who has made one out of the two, they are not to be separated by man."

When we had gone inside we brought up the matter of divorce with Jesus. He put it very simply, "If a man divorces his wife and marries again, he is guilty of adultery against her. In the same way, if a woman divorces her husband and marries again, she is guilty of adultery." (1-12)

One day some parents brought their children to Jesus so he could bless them with his touch. We rebuked the parents, but when Jesus saw what we were doing, he became indignant. "Let the little children come to me!" he told us. "Don't stop them; God's kingdom belongs to the child-like. I assure you that no one will enter the kingdom of God unless they receive it like a little child." Then Jesus gathered the children into his arms, placed his hands on them and blessed them. (13-16)

As Jesus was leaving on a trip, a man came running up and fell to his knees before him. "Good teacher," he exclaimed, "what must I do to earn eternal life?"

"Now why do you call me good?" asked Jesus; "no one is truly good except God?" But to answer your question, the commandments, as you know, say, "Do not murder, do not commit adultery, do not steal, do not give false testimony, do not cheat, honor your father and mother."

"Teacher," the man replied, "I have obeyed those commandments ever since I was a little boy."

With a look of genuine love, Jesus said, "There's one more thing you need to do; go and sell everything you own, then give the money to the poor. That way you will have treasure in heaven. Then come and take up my way of life."

Shocked at such a prospect, the man — who, incidentally, had a huge estate — went away sorrowful. Jesus looked around at us and said, "It's so difficult for the wealthy to enter the kingdom of God!" We could hardly believe what we heard, so once again Jesus said, "It's so difficult for the wealthy to enter the kingdom of God! Without a doubt, it would be easier for a camel to squeeze through the eye of a needle than for a wealthy person to enter the kingdom of God."

That made us even more astounded, so we asked, "Is it possible for anyone to be saved?"

Jesus looked us straight in the eye and said, "What is impossible for man is not for God, because with him everything is possible."

At that point I just had to say something. "We've given up everything we had and become your followers," I exclaimed.

"That's right," said Jesus, "and I assure you that anyone who leaves home, brothers, sisters, mother, father, children or property for my sake and the sake of the gospel, will receive, in this world, a hundred times as much — houses, brothers, sisters, mothers, children and property (all with persecution) — and in the world to come will receive eternal life. But many who now seem to be so important, will at that time be seen as insignificant; and those who now seem to be unimportant will be the most significant." (17-31)

Traveling from the east, the road rises steeply to Jerusalem. Jesus was out front and we disciples were following, astonished at his obvious determination to get there. Others traveling with us sensed the drama and became apprehensive. At one point along the road Jesus took us aside and told us what would happen to him upon arrival.

"Listen," he said, "when we arrive in Jerusalem I will be turned over to the ruling priests and the teachers of religious law. They will condemn me, the Son of Man, to death and turn me over to the Romans who will mock me, spit on me, flog me with a whip, and kill me. But three days later I will rise from the dead." (32-34)

James and John, the sons of Zebedee, approached Jesus and said, "Teacher, there is something we'd like you to do for us."

"What's that?" responded Jesus

"When you're on your royal throne, allow the two of us the honor of sitting, one on your right hand and the other on your left."

"You haven't the faintest idea what that would involve," said Jesus. "Are you able to drink the cup of suffering that I'm about to drink? Are you able to be "baptized" into the suffering and death into which I'm about to be immersed?"

"Yes. We are able," they exclaimed.

Then Jesus said to them, "You will indeed drink the cup I drink and be baptized with the baptism I go through, but it is not for me to say who will sit on my right or my left. Those seats of honor are for those whom God has chosen."

When the rest of us learned what James and John had requested, we were furious. So Jesus called us all together and said to us, "It's common knowledge that in the Gentile world those in charge lord it over their subjects, and that officials make their authority felt. But it's not to be that way with you. Whoever wants to be first, must be the servant of all the others. When I, the Son of Man, came, it was not to be served but to serve by giving my life as a ransom for many." (35-45)

Our route to Jerusalem took us through Jericho. As we were leaving town along with a large crowd, we passed by a blind beggar by the name of Bartimaeus (the son of Timaeus). He was sitting beside the road, and when he heard that Jesus of Nazareth was among the travelers he began to call out, "Jesus, Son of David! Have mercy on me!"

Many in the crowd rebuked him, insisting that he be quiet but he shouted out all the louder, "Son of David! Have mercy on me!"

Jesus stopped. "Tell him to come here," he said to those around him. So they called to the blind man, saying, "Good news! Jesus wants you to come to him, so let's go."

Bartimaeus threw off his robe, jumped to his feet, and made his way to Jesus.

"What do you want me to do for you?" asked Jesus.

"Rabbi," pleaded the blind man, "please help me see again."

And Jesus said to him, "You can go now because you faith is healing you." And at that very moment the beggar's vision was restored and he could see. And as we continued on toward Jerusalem, he followed close behind. (46-52)

Mark Eleven

As we were approaching Jerusalem, Jesus sent two of his disciples on ahead to the villages of Bethphage and Bethany, close by the Mount of Olives. He told them, "Go into that village just ahead of you and as you enter, you will see a young donkey that's never been ridden. It will be tethered, so untie it and bring it to me. Should any one ask you what you are doing, just say, 'The colt is needed for God's service and will be sent back as soon as possible.'"

So the two disciples went into the village and found the colt tied up outside a house. As they were untying the colt, some bystanders questioned, "What are you doing, untying that colt?"

The disciples told them what Jesus had said ("It is needed for God's service"), so the locals let them go ahead. When the disciples returned to Jesus they saddled the colt with their own garments and Jesus mounted it. Many in the crowd took off their cloaks and spread them out on the road. Others did the same with leafy branches they had cut in the fields. As Jesus rode toward Jerusalem, the crowd kept shouting, "Praise be to God! Blessed is the One who comes in the name of the Lord! Blessed is the coming kingdom of our father David! Praise be to God!" (1-10)

When Jesus arrived in Jerusalem, he went to the temple and looked around carefully at everything. Since it was already late, we all returned to the town of Bethany.

The following day on our way to Jerusalem, Jesus became hungry. In the distance he saw a fig tree in leaf so he went to see if it had any fruit. Since it was still early in the season, the tree had produced nothing but leaves. In response, Jesus said to the tree, "May no one ever eat figs from you again!" We took note of what our Teacher said. (11-14)

Once back in Jerusalem, Jesus went immediately to the temple area and began to drive out those who were buying and selling animals for sacrifice. He knocked over the tables of the moneychangers. He scattered the stools of the dove sellers. No one was to use the temple courtyard as a marketplace. Jesus told the people, "In scripture it is written, 'My Temple is to be a house of prayer for all, but you have turned it into a place for thieves to prosper!" When the ruling priests and teachers of religious law heard about this, they began to make final plans on how to get rid of Jesus. They were afraid of him because everybody was fascinated by his teaching.

That evening we all went back out to Bethany. The next morning on our way back to Jerusalem we saw the fig tree that Jesus had cursed. It was completely dead. I remembered what Jesus had done and exclaimed, "Look, Rabbi! The fig tree you cursed is all withered up."

Jesus said to us, "Have faith in God. Believe me when I tell you that if anyone should say to this mountain, 'Get up and be thrown in the sea,' it will happen. However, if that person has any doubt in his heart, it will not happen. That's why I tell you that whenever you pray for something, believe that your prayer is already answered, and sure enough, it will be. But when you stand to pray (as custom has it), you must forgive any grudge you hold against another so that your heavenly Father may forgive all the wrongs you have done." (15-26)

Upon entering Jerusalem we went to the temple area where, as we were walking around, Jesus was approached by a group of ruling priests, teachers of religious law and elders. "By whose authority are you doing all this?" they demanded. "Who gave you permission to teach in this sacred place?"

Jesus told them, "I will ask you a simple question. If you will answer it, I will tell you by what authority I do these things. Who gave John the right to baptize? Was it God or some group of people? Tell me!"

They reasoned among themselves, "If we say that John's authority came from God, he will ask why we refused to believe him. But if we say it came from a human source …?" (They were afraid of what the crowd might do because everyone believed that John was a true prophet.) (27-33)

Mark Twelve

When Jesus addressed the religious authorities he always spoke in parables. This time he said, "Once there was a man who planted a vineyard. He fenced it in, dug a trough to catch the wine, and built a lookout tower. After leasing it out to some tenant farmers, he left on a long journey. When harvest season came, he sent one of his servants to collect his share of the produce. But the tenants grabbed his servant, beat him severely and sent him back empty-handed. So the owner sent a second servant to collect his share. This one was treated disgracefully, beaten over the head. The next servant to go was killed by the tenants. Others were treated the same way; they were thrashed, sometimes so severely that they died. Finally there was only one person left to be sent, the man's own dear son. 'Certainly they will respect my son,' he thought. So, with reluctance, he sent his own son. When the tenant farmers saw this one approaching they said to one another, 'Here comes the heir to the estate. Come on! Let's kill him! Then everything will be ours.' So they grabbed him and murdered him; then they threw his body out of the vineyard.

"Now what do you suppose the owner of the vineyard will do about that?" asked Jesus. "No question but that he'll come and kill that bunch. Then he'll lease out the vineyard to some other farmer. You've read the scripture, haven't you, that says, 'The stone that the builders rejected has become the very cornerstone! We are amazed to see what God has done.'"

The religious authorities would liked to have arrested Jesus, but they were afraid of the crowd so they turned away and left. They were fully aware that the story Jesus told was directed at them. (1-12)

Some Pharisees, along with some cronies of Herod, were sent to trap Jesus into saying something for which they could arrest him. They said, "Teacher, we know that you're a man of integrity. You're not swayed by the opinion of others nor do you show partiality. You truly teach the way of God. So, tell us, 'Is it permissible to pay taxes to Caesar, or is it not? Should we pay them or shouldn't we?'"

Jesus could see through their hypocrisy, so he asked, "Why are you trying to trip me up? Give me a Roman coin so I can examine it." They handed him a denarius and he asked, "Whose image and name are stamped on this coin?

"Caesar's" they answered.

"Well then," said Jesus, "Give to Caesar what belongs to Caesar, and give to God what belongs to God." His answer left them speechless. (13-17)

Some Sadducees (a religious group that claimed no one could rise from the dead) came to Jesus with this question: "Teacher, Moses wrote that if a man dies leaving his wife childless, his brother should marry the widow and have children for his deceased brother. Now suppose there were a family of seven brothers. The oldest took a wife and died without children. So the second brother married the widow and he also died leaving no children. The same thing with the third brother. In fact all seven brothers married her and died without children. Finally, the woman herself died. Now the question is, 'Whose wife will she be when all seven brothers come back to life?

All seven had married her.'"

Jesus replied, "You are mistaken about life after death because you don't understand the teaching of scripture nor have you experienced the power of God. When men and women rise from the dead there is no reason for them to marry; in that way they are like the angels in heaven. Now concerning the dead being raised, have you not read in the writings of Moses how God spoke to Moses at the burning bush and said to him, 'I am the God of Abraham, the God of Isaac, and the God of Jacob?' He is the God of the living, not the dead. You are badly mistaken on the question of life after death." (18-27)

Among those listening to the discussion was a teacher of religious law. He was impressed by how well Jesus had answered the Sadducees, so he stepped forward and asked, "Which of the commandments is the most important?"

Jesus answered, "The most important commandment is this: 'Listen, O Israel! The Lord our God is the one and only God, and you are to love him with all your heart, soul, mind, and strength.' The second important commandment is this, 'You are to love your neighbor as yourself.' There is no commandment more important than these."

"That's right, Teacher!" exclaimed the expert in religious law. "You have spoken the truth. He is the one God, there is no other. To love him with all your heart, understanding, and strength, and to love your neighbor as yourself, is far more important than to fulfill all the ceremonies of religion."

When Jesus saw how thoughtfully the man had responded, he said to him, "You are not far from the kingdom of God." After that no one had the nerve to question Jesus. (28-34)

Jesus remained in the temple, teaching. He asked, "Why do the teachers of religious law hold that the Messiah will be a descendant of King David? It was David himself, inspired by the Holy Spirit, who said, 'The Lord said to my lord, 'Take a seat at my right hand, until I put your enemies under your feet.' Since David himself calls the Messiah, 'my Lord,' how could the Messiah be his descendant?" The crowd was delighted when they heard all that Jesus taught. (35-37)

Jesus also said, "Watch out for those teachers of religious law who enjoy being seen in long flowing robes and greeted with respect in the marketplace. They love being seated in the seats of honor in the synagogues and at the head table at every banquet. Yet they are the ones who cheat widows out of all they have and like to make long prayers in public. These men will be punished more severely.

Jesus sat down near the Temple treasury and watched as people dropped coins into the collection box. Many rich people were throwing in large amounts. Then a poor widow came by and dropped in two little copper coins, worth less than a penny. Jesus called this to our attention saying, "I assure you that this poor widow has put more into the collection box than all the others. That's because they gave only a small part of their wealth, but she gave everything she had, all she had to live on." (38-44)

Mark Thirteen

As Jesus was leaving the Court of the Gentiles through the east gate, one of us went to him and exclaimed, "Master, look at those magnificent buildings and the huge blocks of stone they're made of!"

Jesus responded, "Look again at those wonderful buildings. They will all be demolished; not a single block will be left in place."

Later Jesus was sitting on the Mount of Olives across the Kidron Valley from the temple and four of us (myself, James, John, and Andrew) came to him in private. I asked, "Tell us, when will all this happen? What sort of sign can you give us so we'll know that they are about to take place?"

Jesus warned us against those who would try to deceive us. He said, "Many will claim to speak for me, saying, "I am he," and lead many astray. Don't be alarmed when you hear of wars, both real and threatened. These things must happen but that doesn't mean that the end has finally come. Nations will continue to war against each another; kingdoms will attack one other. There will be earthquakes in various parts of the world, and a scarcity of food. These are the beginning of birth pains. You must be on your guard! The authorities will turn you over to local Jewish law courts and you will be beaten in their synagogues. You will stand trial before provincial governors and kings, but this will provide you the opportunity to tell them about me. But before the end comes the gospel must be preached to all people. So when you are arrested and taken to court, don't worry ahead of time about what to say. In situations like this God will tell you exactly what to say. In fact, it won't be you speaking, but the Holy Spirit." (1-11)

"Brothers will hand over their own brothers to be killed, and fathers their own children. Young people will rise up against their parents and have them put to death. You will be hated by everyone, because of me. Only those who never turn back will be saved. The day will come when you will see the 'abomination of desolation' standing in the sacred place where he should not be. (Pay careful attention to this.) That's when those in Judea should go quickly to the hill country for places to hide. If someone is up on the roof, he shouldn't waste time going down into the house to gather his belongings. If he is out in the field he shouldn't come back in to get something else to wear. It will be terrible for women who are pregnant or nursing when all this happens. And pray that your flight for safety won't be in winter."

"Those will be days of distress greater than the world has ever known since the beginning of God's creation. And there never will be anything like it again. Unless the Lord shortens the number of those days, no one will survive. However, for the sake of those he has chosen, the Christian community, he has shortened that time. In those days if anyone says to you, 'Look, here is the Messiah!' or 'There he is!' don't believe him, for false messiahs and false prophets will show up and perform signs and wonders. Their goal is to deceive, if possible, the very ones God has chosen. So be on your guard! I have told you ahead of time what will happen." (12-23)

"But something even worse is yet to come. In the days that follow that time of suffering, the sun will grow dark and the moon will give no light. The stars will fall from the sky and the heavens will be shaken. At that point everyone will see the Son of Man descending on the clouds with great power and glory. That is when he will send out his angels to gather his chosen ones from the four winds, from the ends of the earth to the ends of heaven."

"Here is a lesson you can learn from the fig tree. When its branches become tender and begin to sprout leaves, you know that summer is just around the corner. In the same way, when that period of great distress begins (and I've just described it), you will know that the temple is about to be destroyed. What I tell you is true. Everything I have told you will happen before the people who are now alive, die. Heaven and earth will disappear, but what I say will remain forever. However no one will know the exact time, not even the angelic hosts or even the Son himself. No one but the Father knows that. So stay on watch; we simply do not know when the time will come."

"This entire scenario is like a man who took a long journey, leaving his affairs in the hands of his servants. He gave specific instructions to each one and told the gatekeeper to watch for his return. Like the gatekeeper, you too must keep watch. You never know when the Son of Man will return. It could be in the evening, or later around midnight, or perhaps before dawn or daybreak. If you don't watch, he might arrive and find you sleeping. What I say now to you, I say to everyone: Stay awake." (24-37)

Mark Fourteen

It was now only two days before the Festival of Passover and Unleavened Bread. The chief priests and teachers of religious law were planning to take Jesus by stealth and put him to death, but they knew they shouldn't try it during the Festival lest it cause a riot.

Jesus was in the town of Bethany at the house of Simon, a man cured of leprosy. A woman carrying an alabaster jar full of very expensive ointment (it was made from pure nard) came in where they were eating. She opened the jar and poured its contents on Jesus' head. Some of those watching became indignant and sneered, "Why waste all that expensive ointment? It could have been sold for more than a year's wages and the money given to the poor." They were actually angry at her.

But Jesus said, "Leave her alone! Why criticize her for doing such a thoughtful thing? She did what was hers to do; she anointed my body ahead of time for burial. Wherever the story of my life, especially these last days, is told anywhere in the world, what she has done will be remembered." (1-9)

At this point, one of the disciples, Judas Iscariot, left and went to the chief priests to offer them his help in taking Jesus into custody. Of course they were delighted to hear this, and promised to pay him for his trouble. So Judas kept watching for just the right moment to betray his master.

On the first day of the Festival of Unleavened Bread (that's when the Passover lamb is sacrificed) we asked Jesus where he wanted us to prepare the Passover meal for him. He sent two of his disciples to Jerusalem with the following instructions: "As you enter the city you will be met by a man carrying a water jar. Follow him. When he enters a house, say to the owner, 'The Teacher would like to know where the guest room is in which he and his disciples are to eat their Passover meal.' Then the man will take you to a large upstairs room all ready for the occasion. That's where you are to prepare our Passover meal." The two disciples left for the city and found everything just as Jesus had told them. So they prepared the Passover meal. (10-16)

When evening came, Jesus and the twelve of us went to the man's house. As they were eating, Jesus said, "I tell you the truth, one of you is going to betray me — one who is sharing this very meal. We were upset and one after another kept saying, "Surely you don't mean me, do you?"

Jesus answered, "Yes, it is one of you, one of my own disciples, one who is dipping his bread into the same bowl with me. The Son of Man must die, just as the Scriptures teach, but how terrible for that one who will betray me. It would have been better for him if he'd never been born."

While we were eating, Jesus took a loaf of unleavened bread, gave thanks and broke it in pieces. He gave a piece to each of us, saying "Take it, it is my body." Then he poured a cup of wine, gave thanks and handed it to us, saying, "This is my blood, the blood of the covenant, poured out as a sacrifice for many." We all drank from the cup.

Then Jesus said, "I tell you the truth, I will not

drink wine again until that day when I drink the new wine of the kingdom of God." Then, after singing a hymn, we left for the Mount of Olives. (17-26)

On the way, Jesus said, "All of you will desert me, because in scripture God says, 'I will strike the shepherd, and the sheep will be scattered.' But after I am raised from the dead, I will go ahead of you into Galilee."

Shocked by this, I said to Jesus, "I will never leave you, even though all the others do!"

Jesus replied, "I tell you the truth, Peter, this very night, before the rooster crows a second time, you will have denied three times that you know me."

"No," I replied emphatically. "Even if I must die with you, I will not say I've never known you!" And the rest of the disciples joined me in the same vow. (27-31)

We came to an olive orchard across the Kidron Valley from Jerusalem. It was called Gethsemane.

Jesus told the other disciples to wait there while he went a bit further to pray, but James, John and I were to go with him. He began to pray and soon became distressed and deeply troubled. He said, "My soul is so crushed with sorrow that I could die. Stay with me and keep watch. Then he went aside and, falling to the ground, prayed that if it were possible he might not have to go through the suffering that lay ahead. "Abba, Father," he cried out, "nothing is impossible for you, so take this cup of suffering from me. Yet I want your will to be done, not mine."

Then Jesus came back and found the three of us asleep. He said to me, "Simon, are you still sleeping? Couldn't you have stayed awake for even one hour? Stay awake and pray that you won't fail in the coming trial. You always want to do the right thing but you don't have the strength to do it." Once again Jesus left and prayed as he did before. Then he came back and again we were asleep, our eyes so heavy that we simply couldn't stay awake. We had no excuse. Later, when he joined us for the third time, he said, "Is it possible that you are still sleeping? Enough of that! The time has come for the Son of Man to be betrayed into the hands of sinners. Get up! Let's go. Look, my betrayer is already here." (32-42)

While Jesus was still speaking, Judas, one of the Twelve, arrived with a group of men sent by the religious hierarchy, the ruling priests, teachers of religious law, and elders. They were armed with swords and clubs. According to the plan, the betrayer would identify Jesus with a kiss. So Judas went up to Jesus, greeted him with "Rabbi," and kissed him. Then the men grabbed Jesus and held him so he couldn't get away. One man standing there drew his sword and swung it at the servant of the High Priest, cutting off his ear.

"Why have you come with swords and clubs to arrest me," asked Jesus. "Did you think that I was planning a revolution? If so, why didn't you arrest me in the temple courts; I was there teaching, day after day? No, all this has happened to fulfill what the scriptures say about me." At this point we disciples deserted him and ran away. (43-52)

With Jesus in custody, the mob headed for the house of the high priest where the ruling priests, elders, and teachers of the Law had gathered. Following along behind was a young man, wearing nothing but a loose linen sheet. They tried to grab him, but he managed to escape, slipping out of the sheet and running away naked. I had been following some distance behind, but when we arrived I went right into the high priest's courtyard and joined the guards warming themselves around an open fire. The ruling priests and the entire Council had gathered upstairs and were searching for some kind of evidence against Jesus so they could put him to death. They came up with nothing. A number of witnesses spoke against Jesus but their testimonies were contradictory.

Then others stood up and offered false testimony against Jesus. "We heard him say, 'I'm going to tear down this temple made by man, and in three days build one that man could never build.'" Yet they couldn't agree even on this.

At this point, the high priest stood up in their midst and, addressing Jesus, asked, "Are you going to answer the accusations made by these men, or are you not?" Jesus remained silent; he didn't say a word.

Then the high priest posed this crucial question, "Are you the Messiah, the Son of the Blessed One?" And Jesus answered, "I am. What's more, you will all see the Son of Man seated at the right hand of the Mighty One and coming on the clouds of heaven!" At this the high priest tore his garments and said, "Why do we need any other witnesses? You have all heard him blaspheme. What's your verdict?"

"Guilty!" they shouted. "Put him to death!" Some of high court began to spit on Jesus. They put a blindfold on him and hitting him with their fists jeered, "Who hit you that time?"

Then they turned him over to the guards who joined in the abuse. (53-65)

Meanwhile, I was down below in the courtyard. One of the servant girls who worked for the high priest came by and noticed me there by the fire. She looked at me carefully and said, "You were one of the men with Jesus the Nazarene."

I denied it, saying, "I haven't the faintest idea what you're talking about." Then I slipped out into the entryway — and a rooster crowed.

The servant girl saw me there and once again said to those standing around, "This man belongs to that group." I denied it again.

A short while later some men standing there challenged me, "You must be one of them, for you're a Galilean just like the others."

I began to call down damnation. With an oath I swore, "I know nothing of this man you're talking about!" At that very moment a rooster crowed for the second time and I remembered what Jesus had said to me: "Before the rooster crows twice you will have disowned me three times." I broke down and wept. (66-72)

Mark Fifteen

Early in the morning the leading priests met as the high Council (the elders and the teachers of religious law were there) and planned their next step. Then they bound Jesus and took him to Pilate, the Roman official in charge of Judea. Pilate asked, "Are you the king of the Jews?" Jesus answered, "Yes, but not as you mean it." The leading priests brought all sorts of accusations against Jesus, so Pilate asked again, "Are you not going to answer? You heard all the charges brought against you." Jesus wouldn't say a word and it left Pilate dumbfounded.

It was the governor's custom at Passover to release a single prisoner to the Jews; it could be anyone they wanted. At that time there was a group of men in prison for an insurrection involving murder. One of them was a man by the name of Barabbas. The crowd went up to Pilate's palace and asked him, as they did every year, to release a prisoner. Pilate asked, "Would you like me to turn over this 'king of the Jews?'" He was fully aware that they had arrested Jesus because he was a threat to their authority. But the priests incited the crowd to demand that Barabbas be released. So Pilate said, "And what do you want me to do with this man you call the king of the Jews?"

"Crucify him!" they shouted. "Crucify him!"
"Why?" objected Pilate. "What crime has he committed?" But the crowd kept shouting all the louder, "Crucify him! Crucify him!"

So Pilate, wishing to appease the crowd, released Barabbas to them. Then he had Jesus scourged and turned over to be crucified. The guards on duty took him into the barracks of the governor's palace (the Praetorium) and called together the rest of their battalion. They dressed Jesus in a purple robe, twisted some thorny branches into a crown and jammed it on his head. Then they mocked him, saying, "Hail! King of the Jews!" They took a staff and beat him on the head. They spit on him. They dropped to their knees and honored him as though he were royalty. When they grew tired of their fun, they ripped off the purple robe and put his clothes back on. Then they took him out to be crucified.

(1-20)

On their way out of Jerusalem, they met Simon, a member of the Jewish community in Cyrene, as he was returning from the countryside. (Simon was the father of Alexander and Rufus.) The soldiers ordered him to carry the cross beam that Jesus had been carrying. The soldiers brought Jesus to a place called Golgotha (which means "The Place of the Skull"). Some women offered him wine flavored with myrrh to dull the pain but he refused it. Then, after stripping Jesus of his clothes (they threw dice to see who would get what), the soldiers nailed him to the cross. It was nine o'clock in the morning. The accusation posted against him read, "The King of the Jews."

On either side of Jesus they crucified another "revolutionary," one on his right and one on his left. The crowd that was around the cross ridiculed Jesus, wagging their heads and taunting, "Look at you now! You said you could destroy the Temple and rebuild it in three days! So, why don't you just jump down from the cross and save yourself!" Even the religious leaders mocked Jesus among themselves, saying, "He came to save others, but he can't save himself. Let's watch this Messiah, this self-appointed king of Israel, step down from the cross. If that happens we could believe." (21-32)

At noon a strange darkness settled over the entire land of Judea and remained for the next three hours. Then at three o'clock Jesus cried out in a loud voice, "Eloi, Eloi, lema sabachthani?" (that means, "My God, my God, why have you forsaken me?"). Some of those standing there heard him and said, "Listen, he's calling for Elijah." One of them soaked a sponge with cheap vinegar wine and lifted it up on a staff so Jesus could wet his mouth. "Let's keep watch," he said, "then we can see if Elijah will come and take him off the cross."

At that point Jesus cried out in a loud voice and took his last breath. The veil separating the courtyard from the Holy Place was torn apart, top to bottom. When the Roman commander saw how Jesus had died, he confessed, "Surely, this man was the Son of God." Some women were watching from a distance. Among them were Mary Magdalene, Mary (the mother of James the

Younger), and Salome. When Jesus was ministering in Galilee, these women had been with him, caring for his needs. Among the many women were those who had come to Jerusalem with him for Passover. (33-41)

It was the day of Preparation (that is, the day before the Sabbath). So as evening approached, Joseph of Arimathea, a respected member of the Council, who was looking forward to the coming of God's kingdom, went boldly to Pilate and asked for the body of Jesus. Pilate was surprised to learn that Jesus had died so quickly, so he asked Joseph how long it had been. When the Roman officer on duty confirmed that Jesus had died, Pilate gave permission. Joseph took the body down from the cross and wrapped it in some linen cloth that he had purchased. Then he laid it in a tomb that had been carved out of rock. Across the opening he rolled a stone. Mary Magdalene and Mary the mother of Jesus took careful note of where the body was laid.

Mark Sixteen

That evening when the Sabbath was over, Mary Magdalene, Mary the mother of James, and Salome went out and bought some aromatic spices so they could anoint the body of Jesus. Very early Sunday morning, at sunrise, they went to the tomb. On the way they were questioning one another, "Who will be able to roll away such a huge stone from the entrance of the tomb?" However, when they arrived they saw that it had already been removed. They entered the tomb and saw a young man sitting on the right side, dressed in white. The women were terrified? " Don't be frightened" the angel said. "I know you've come to find Jesus of Nazareth, the man who was crucified, but he isn't here! He has risen from the dead! Look, right there is where they laid his body. What you are to do is to go and tell his disciples (and he mentioned me, Peter, by name), that Jesus is going on ahead of you to Galilee, and will meet you there just as he said." Frightened out of their wits, the women fled from the tomb. They said nothing to anyone because they were too afraid. (1-8)

Long Ending

The first person to see Jesus after he arose from the dead on Sunday morning was Mary Magdalene, the woman from whom he had cast seven demons. She came to us who were in tears mourning our loss and told us what had happened. When she said that Jesus was alive and that she had seen him, we didn't believe her.

After this, Jesus appeared in a different form to two of his followers as they were on their way from Jerusalem into the country. They hurried back and told the rest of us but we didn't believe them either.

After that he appeared to eleven of us while we were eating. He rebuked us for our incredulity and hardness of heart in not believing those who had seen him alive.

Then he told us to go everywhere in the entire world and proclaim the Good News to everyone. He said. "Whoever believes and is baptized will be saved, but whoever refuses to believe will be condemned. Those who believe will be given the power to perform miracles. In my name, they will cast out demons. They will speak in new languages. They will be able to pick up snakes with their hands, and if they drink any deadly poison it will not harm them. When they lay their hands on the sick, the sick will get well."

Then, when the Lord had finished speaking with us, he was taken up into heaven and took his place at the right hand of God. We disciples went everywhere proclaiming the Good News, and the Lord worked with us, confirming what we said with many miraculous signs. (9-20)

Made in the USA
Lexington, KY
21 December 2019